The People's History

Houghton-le-Spring

by

Geoffrey Berriman

White Lion Corner. Houghton-le-Spring 8919

The White Lion on the corners of Newbottle Street and Sunderland Street in the 1920s. This fine early 18th century building was much photographed for postcards in the early part of the 20th century. It is recorded in the early 19th century that the Magistrates held their court in the White Lion on alternate Thursdays.

Previous page: Herbert Bentley, Paperhanger and Painter, and staff, *circa* 1912. The premises stood near the Lake Entrance, Sunderland Street. 'The Lake' was an artificial boating lake created in the late 19th century and although it was filled in before the end of that century the site continued to be known as 'The Lake'.

Copyright © Geoffrey Berriman 2000

First published in 2000 by

The People's History Ltd
Suite 1
Byron House
Seaham Grange Business Park
Seaham
Co. Durham SR7 0PY

ISBN 1 902527 19 4

Contents

Houghton Nomads rugby team in 1891.

Introduction

In his *History and Antiquities of the County Palatine of Durham*, published in 1820, Robert Surtees wrote that Houghton-le-Spring was, 'An irregular Village, stretching nearly half a mile in length, and containing several handsome buildings, lies at the head of a fine vale, opening to the South and West, and sheltered on the North and East by a high chain of limestone hills.'

Since the time of Surtees' description Houghton has grown greatly and the word 'Village' has not been an appropriate description for many years. It saw a transformation from a predominantly agricultural community to a time when for some one hundred and fifty years the colliery became the heart of the community. Today, it is, perhaps, still facing the uncertainties of the post-coal era, but it remains an important town with strong evidence of a community spirit and a history of which it can well be proud.

A view of Houghton-le-Spring showing the gasometers in 1906.

Acknowledgements

This is the second book in The People's History Series with which I have been involved, and again I have been fortunate in the number of people who have lent me photographs and postcards, or who have helped me in other ways. I would like to thank the following, and if I have omitted anyone from my list I do apologise for this:

Beamish Museum; Bethany Christian Centre; Mr Drummond Brown; Miss Jean Campbell; Mrs Cansfield; The Dowager Lady Chapman; Mrs E. Clark; Mr D.M. Colling; Mrs Moyra Coxon; Mr Bill Curry; Mrs Freda Denby; Mr A. Dickinson; Mrs E. Dobson; Durham County Records Office; Mrs M.M. Elmes; The Reverend Canon Peter Fisher; Mr Norman Forster; Mrs Bunty Gibson; Mr & Mrs P. Hall; Mr Fraser Kemp MP; Mr Harry Lax; Houghton Comrades Club; Houghton-le-Spring Golf Club; Northeast Press Limited; Mrs Carol Oliver; Mr J.G. Robson; Mrs M. Poulter; Mr & Mrs W. Richardson; Mr D. Sangster; Scholastic Electronics; Dr J.A. Sinclair; Mrs M. Tease; Mr Arthur Veitch; The Reverend Dr Ian Wallis and the PCC of St Michael and All Angels; Mrs Jean Wilkins; Mr Alan Yardley; the headteachers of St Michaels' RC Primary, Davenport, Gillas Lane Primary, Burnside Primary and Bernard Gilpin Primary Schools.

I should like to thank Mr George Nairn for providing photographs and for his expert advice and Mrs Lena Cooper, co-author with me on the book *Fencehouses, Lambton, Burnmoor & Chilton Moor* in The People's History Series for her encouragement. As in the earlier book I would like to pay tribute to the late Mr Ken Richardson for his pioneering work in the production of photographic histories of the Houghton area. I should also like to thank all those Houghton people who approached me in a friendly manner when I was taking photographs for the book.

Houghton-le-Spring Town Band outside the Queen's Head public house, Sunderland Street, *circa* 1900. The Queen's Head was known locally as 'The Pillars'.

THE TOWN OF HOUGHTON-LE-SPRING

Point Duty in The Broadway, 1924. Note the tram on the left and the buses on the right.

A view of the town from the top of the church tower, 1935. The colliery can be seen in the background. Most of the buildings on the right side of the photograph have been demolished.

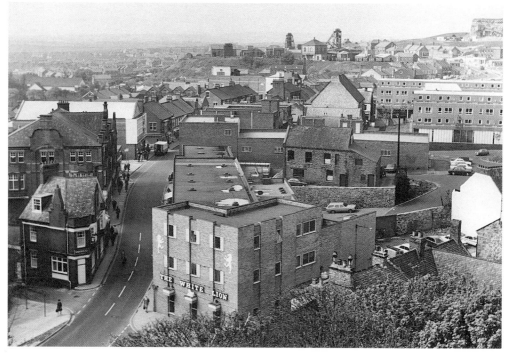

Another view of the town, taken in 1972. Again, the colliery is prominent in the background. The Mautland Square Flats, built in the late 1960s, can be seen at the top right of the picture as they were before being reduced in height and converted into the shopping units that exist today.

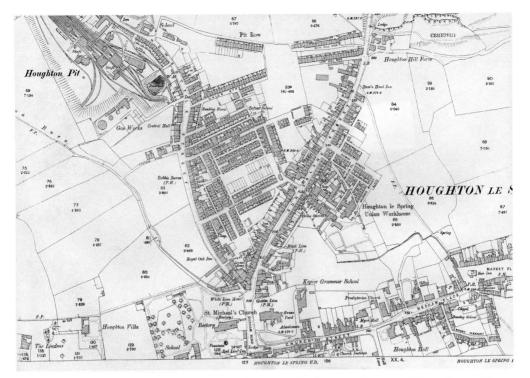

The extract above reproduced from the 1896 Ordnance Survey Map shows the town centre before the building of the west side of Newbottle Street. Compare with the extract below, reproduced from the 1939 Ordnance Survey Map, showing a large amount of additional housing.

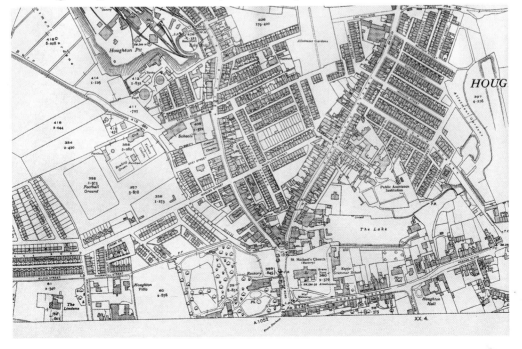

Rainton Bridge and Durham Road reproduced from the 1896 Ordnance Survey Map. Rainton Corn Mill is marked bottom left.

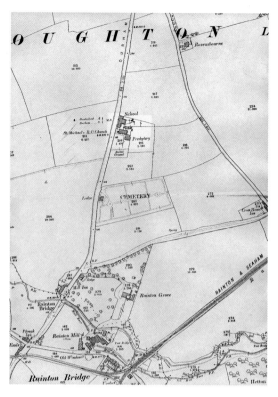

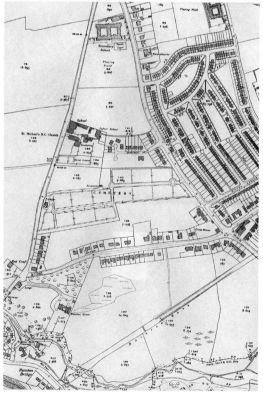

Reproduced from the 1939 Ordnance Survey Map. By this stage Rainton Corn Mill had been demolished, and a great deal of new house building had taken place.

A march passing through The Broadway in the 1930s. One of the banners reads, 'We want work or full maintenance – demonstration'.

A Newbottle Street scene in the 1960s after the building of the new post office and the conversion of the Coliseum Cinema into the Fine Fare Supermarket (now Superdrug).

A view of Sunderland Street, *circa* 1920.

Newbottle Street, *circa* 1930. The middle building on the left is the Newcastle Arms public house.

Houghton Cut, *circa* 1920.

Houghton Cut, 2000. The road has been considerably widened to take the A690 dual carriageway from Sunderland to Durham.

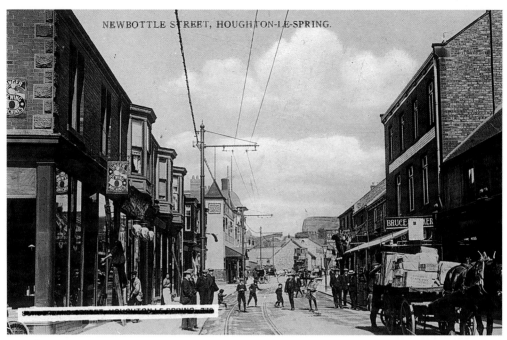

Newbottle Street in 1916. Compare this photograph with the following two.

Newbottle Street, *circa* 1956. Note the location of the former post office building on the left which subsequently became a branch of the Midland Bank, and which is now Stanley Racing.

Newbottle Street in 2000.

This photograph from the collection of Beamish Museum is described as 'Slum Clearance Area 27th September 1935', but it has been difficult to identify the precise location. It could be the New Town area along Seaham Road. Does any reader know? The three houses at the front are particularly old and are roofed with clay pantiles which were traditionally used before slates became widely available in the area in the latter half of the 19th century.

The Market Building including H.P. Tyler's shoe shop, *circa* 1905. In the 19th century the building also served as the Town Hall.

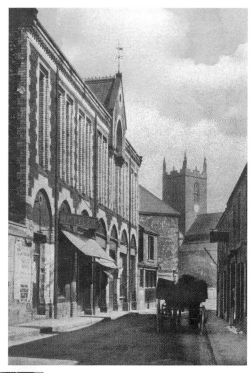

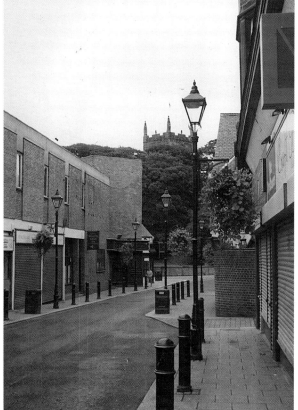

This photograph was taken in 2000 from a similar position to the one above. The shops on the left replaced the Market Building in the late 1960s.

Sunderland Street in 1916. Compare this with the photograph below taken in 2000. This street was very prominent containing many shops and businesses, but the major part of it was demolished in the 1960s to make way for the new Sunderland/Durham Road. Buildings in the top photograph which survive today include those shown below on the left now containing the hair dressing salon, Dinabite, Flynn's Bar and the May Ho Chinese takeaway.

The 'Bus Stand' in The Broadway, *circa* 1927.

A photograph of the same location in 2000. Note that The King's Hall shown as having five storeys in the photograph above has been reduced to two.

A photograph showing the church end of The Broadway at the end of a school day in 1999. This was before the completion of the paving works shown in the photograph below.

This photograph looking towards the old Red Lion building was taken in 2000 after the completion of the extensive paving works in The Broadway.

Aged Miner's Home's, Houghton-le-Spring. 8910

The Aged Miners' Homes, *circa* 1930. The twelve cottages were built in 1926. It was usual for commemorative stones to be laid by local dignitaries when Aged Miners' Homes were built and a number can be seen on these cottages. A stone which can be seen on No 1 lists the names of the Homes Committee responsible for the building.

A view of the Aged Miners' Homes in 2000.

A view of Nesham Place, often spelt Neasham in the past, *circa* 1916. The Methodist Church can be seen on the left. The building in the right foreground was formerly the Wheatsheaf public house. The scene can be compared with the photograph below taken in 2000. The Methodist Church has been demolished and the Wheatsheaf is now a private house.

A group of Houghton men in Newbottle Street in the early 1960s. It is believed that the man with the crutches was the focus of attention because he was injured on his last day of work at the pit before retirement, never having been injured before.

A view of The Broadway looking towards the Red Lion, *circa* 1959.

This building in Vine Place can be found behind the bustle of Newbottle Street. Now derelict, it once formed a pair of cottages until the 1960s. Mr G.D. Rose carried out his gentlemen's hairdressing business in the right hand cottage, and the left hand cottage was used for a time as a vet's surgery until relatively recently.

Another old building in Vine Place. Still used, it houses the offices of Mr John Waugh, architect, and WCF Fuels Ltd.

The building on the right is the former Red Lion Inn which closed in the late 1970s. A substantial building, it is occupied today by Moody, Stappard & Hill, estate agents; G. Whitfield Ltd, chemists; and G. Elsbury & Co, solicitors.

Church Street with Houghton Hall in the background, 1999.

Some pleasant buildings such as these remain in Church Street, but in the *The Penguin Buildings of England, County Durham 2nd Edition* by Nikolaus Pevsner and revised by Elizabeth Williamson it is stated that: 'The centre of Houghton is now split by part of a giant road system ... Before the dual carriageways in whichever direction one took from the church there were buildings to examine and enjoy. Although a few worthwhile ones survive close to the church, the old centre has been cut short only a few hundred yards south and east of the churchyard.'

Hetton Road in the 1920s.

Compare this photograph taken in 2000 with the photograph above. The road has been widened and trees have grown to obscure some of the housing.

A view of Sunderland Street in 1911.

Looking towards the Market Place in 2000. The middle building on the left was formerly the Wheatsheaf public house.

Newbottle Street, *circa* 1930, showing the White Lion, and next to it the Old Town Hall which contained shops and a billiard hall. The stone wall on the left next to the Britannia public house surrounded the Rectory Garden, now the public park.

Compare this photograph taken in 2000 with the photograph above. The Britannia remains a well known public house in Newbottle Street, but the old White Lion and the Town Hall building were demolished in the late 1960s.

SOME WELL KNOWN HOUGHTON CITIZENS

Tommy Bell of Houghton-le-Spring, Durham.

Tommy Bell of Houghton-le-Spring from a print in *The Table Book* of 1827. In an accompanying article he was described as an: '… eccentric, good humoured character – a lover of a chirruping cup – and a favourite of the pitmen of Durham. He dresses like them and mixes and jokes with them.' In the background of the print can be seen the Parish Church which then had a spire.

A photograph taken in about 1880 of Mrs Grey, the wife of The Honourable and Reverend John Grey who was Rector of Houghton for forty-eight years – 1847-95.

John Legge in about 1880. He was a solicitor and clerk to the Board of Health, the Magistrates, and the Guardians who were the forerunners of the modern day Local Authorities.

John Wilson became the first Member of Parliament for Houghton-le-Spring in 1885. He sat as a Liberal. He began work at the age of 10 in Stanhope Quarries and, at the age of 13, became a coal miner. For several years he worked as a seaman and also worked in the USA from 1863-67. In 1869 he helped to establish the Durham Miners' Association. In 1910 he was awarded the Honorary Degree of Doctor of Civil Law by the University of Durham and he is shown here in his academic robes. He lost his seat as MP for Houghton-le-Spring after only a year, but later became MP for Durham 1890-1915.

John Wilson was succeeded by a Conservative, Nicholas Wood, who sat until 1892, when he lost his seat to a Liberal, Henry Thomas Fenwick. Henry Fenwick sat until 1895, and served subsequently in the Boer War, being awarded the Distinguished Service Order.

Henry Fenwick was succeeded by another Liberal, Robert Cameron, who became the Member for Houghton at the age of 70, and who sat for eighteen years. Robert Cameron had been a headmaster for many years, and had served as a Councillor and Alderman in Sunderland.

In 1913 Robert Cameron was succeeded by Thomas Edward Wing, Liberal. Thomas Wing had been a commercial traveller. In his entry in *Who's Who* he said he had also 'roughed it as an errand boy'.

Houghton's first Labour MP was Robert Richardson who served from 1918-1931. He had been a miner and an Alderman on Durham County Council.

Robert Chapman, National Unionist, defeated Robert Richardson at the General Election of 1931. He had a distinguished military and civic career. In the First World War he had commanded the 4th Durham Howitzer Battalion and 250th Brigade, Royal Field Artillery, being awarded the Distinguished Service Order. He also received numerous other decorations in both World Wars. In 1958 he was created a baronet. He lost his seat in 1935 to William Joseph Stewart, who served as Labour MP until 1945.

Below: William (Bill) Blyton, Labour MP, 1945-64. After his retirement from the House of Commons he was created a Life Peer and sat regularly in the House of Lords. (Photograph: NorthEast Press Ltd, Sunderland Echo.)

The Rt Hon Thomas Urwin, Labour MP, 1964-83. He was leader of the British Parliamentary Delegation to Europe from 1976 until 1979 and also served as a Minister of State from 1968 until 1970. He was appointed a Privy Counsellor. (Photograph: NorthEast Press Ltd, Sunderland Echo.)

Roland Boyes became the Labour MP for the new constituency of Houghton and Washington in 1983, serving until 1997. He was also a Member of the European Parliament from 1979-84. (Photograph: NorthEast Press Ltd, Sunderland Echo.)

Fraser Kemp, Labour, succeeded Roland Boyes as MP in 1997. He was National General Co-ordinator for the Labour Party from 1994-96.

Below: Frank Glen (left) and William (Bill) Brown (right) were partners in the old established firm of solicitors, Legge & Miller, whose offices have been in Sunderland Street for over 150 years. They are shown here shortly before their retirement from the firm in 1984.

HOUGHTON BUILDINGS OF NOTE

PARSONAGE-HOUSE at HOUGHTON-LE-SPRING

A print, *circa* 1820, of the Parsonage House, Houghton-le-Spring. Better known as the Old Rectory, it was converted into offices for Houghton-le-Spring Urban District Council shortly after the Second World War, and now serves as part of Sunderland City Council's Houghton Office.

In the 16th century the building was described as being, 'like a bishop's palace, and far superior to many palaces.' It was rebuilt in the 17th century apart from the west tower, but remained a substantial building in large grounds.

Rainton Mill, *circa* 1890. This was a substantial Corn Mill near Rainton Bridge. The 1896 Ordnance Survey shows a large range of buildings and water works as well as the site of an old windmill.

Rainton Mill has been long demolished, but not far from its site stands the fine early 19th century house, Rainton Grove. This photograph is *circa* 1910.

The Old Rectory in 1952, only a few years after the building had been converted from being the Rectory to offices for Houghton-le-Spring Urban District Council.

The Old Rectory in 1999. The ornate heads of the rainwater downcomers, which can just be seen in the photograph, are inscribed with the date 1794. The right hand part of the building shown in the photograph above has been demolished.

The Old Brewery, also showing the Imperial Garage, in the 1960s. After brewing ceased it was used for some years by Roughts, Skin Merchants and in the 1970s part of it was occupied by a nightclub and wine bar.

The Old Brewery has now been skilfully converted into apartments. This photograph was taken in 1999 during construction work.

The Kepier Building, 2000. In 1574 a Foundation Charter appointed Bernard
Gilpin and John Heath as the first governors of the, 'Free Grammar School and
Almshouse of Kepier in Houghton-le-Spring, in the County of Durham.' In his
History of the County Palatine of Durham (Volume 1 published 1820), Surtees
reported that, 'The school and school house stand on rising ground at the
north east side of the churchyard. The school is a plain building with walls at
least three feet thick.' Part of the building shown in the photograph belongs to
the 1574 foundation, but later there were some 17th century additions. The
school continued until the early part of the 20th century, and was attended by
the sons of many well known families. The building is still in use, and
contains flats and business premises.

The Almshouses in about 1960. They were built in the 17th century by George
Lilburne of Offerton and George Davenport, Rector of Houghton-le-Spring
1664-67, and are still lived in today.

The Welfare Hall in 2000. It was opened in 1931 and regularly used for civic activities. It now forms part of a local authority sports and leisure complex.

Houghton Police Station, Dairy Lane, in the late 1940s. It was built in the 1930s, the previous police station being situated in William Street which was behind Sunderland Street.

This attractive three storey building in Church Street, formerly housing the Catholic Institute, now contains the offices of Hodgson & Coulthard, solicitors. The lamps have been erected in recent years to blend in sympathetically with the architecture.

Laburnum House, a largely Georgian building in Nesham Place taken in 1999.

A print made in about 1840 of Nesham Hall Academy in Nesham Place. The Academy was one of several private schools in the town, some of them taking boarding pupils. The Academy stood on the site now occupied by the Nursery School and the former Bethany Church.

The Manor House, Nesham Place in 1999. Originally a farm house dating back to at least 1795, it has been the home of several well known local medical practitioners, and many older residents will remember surgeries being held there.

Heatherlea House, another fine Georgian house in Nesham Place.

Nos 16 and 18 Market Place. This excellent stone building is probably 18th century. The Market Place was an ancient and prominent area before the expansion of the town in the Newbottle and Sunderland Street areas, and it included a variety of attractive looking housing and inns in a village type setting. The Market Place name is still used for the area today, although it is much changed following a large Local Authority house building programme in the 1950s.

The Copt Hill public house in 2000. It is prominently sited near the road to Seaham. In the 1850s it was listed in *Whelan's Township Directory* as one of twenty-three taverns, inns and hotels, in the town. At that time the Copt Hill was run by a landlady, Elizabeth Willis.

The Mill in Durham Road, 2000. This is another well known public house in the town. It is known to have existed in 1825, but might have earlier origins.

The Burn Inn, Hetton Road, built on the site of the former Cross House, so called, no doubt, because it stood at the crossroads. Cross House Farm stood on the opposite side of the road and some of the farm buildings can still be seen.

The Spring Inn, Market Place, previously the Market Tavern, dating from the late 19th century. There was formerly an open spring in the Market Place and this was clearly marked on 19th century Ordnance Survey Maps, although it has long been culverted. In the mid 19th century, six inns were recorded as trading in the Market Place. These were: the Black Horse, George and Dragon, the Jolly Farmer, the Malsters' Arms, the Sun and the Wheatsheaf, none of which exists today.

The Golden Lion, Sunderland Street, in 2000. The pub dates back to at least the 18th century and is a well preserved example of an inn of its period. It is the only original 'Lion' public house in the town still in use as a pub today. The old White Lion, now demolished, and the Red Lion building, now in use as shops and offices, are featured elsewhere in this book. There was also a Black Lion in Sunderland Street. To the left of the Golden Lion is the building which has been the office for over 150 years of Legge & Miller, solicitors.

Taken in 2000 this photograph shows the back of the Golden Lion including nearest to camera the building which would have been used for stabling.

SHOPS AND THE WORKPLACE

The photographs in this chapter show some of the shops and workplaces in the town from the late 19th century to the present day. Entries for Houghton in 19th century trade directories list a wide variety of businesses. In the mid 19th century, thirteen tailors, sixteen boot and shoemakers, twenty-seven grocers and nine butchers were recorded in the town. The photograph on this page is of Sutheran's Mineral Water Works in Hopper Street, *circa* 1900. Hopper Street lay between Sunderland Street and Newbottle Street.

W. Bassett's Fish and Chip Saloon in Sunderland Street, *circa* 1905.

Mr and Mrs Fish outside their grocery store in Newbottle Lane (now Houghton Road), *circa* 1920. Mr Fish had been blinded in a pit accident.

Premises of William Robinson, grocer, Sunderland Street on 2nd April 1912, the day after they had been wrecked and looted by strikers.

The Gaiety Temperance Bar, Newbottle Street, owned by Alexandro and Colombo Riano who are pictured in the doorway, *circa* 1915.

Unloading goods for Davison's shop at The Quays, Church Street, *circa* 1890. The Quays were the pavement area above road level.

W. Wilson, butcher, 15 Church Street, *circa* 1905.

Adamson's saddlery and harness making shop in Church Street, *circa* 1905.

Interior of Mortons, printers, in Newbottle Street, circa 1915. The building now houses Barclays Bank.

Kay's boot shop in Sunderland Street, *circa* 1920.

Davidson's grocery shop in Edwin Street, *circa* 1920.

H.P. Tyler's shoe shop in Newbottle Street.

R. Grayson, butcher, in the New Market, Newbottle Street, *circa* 1930. The market was demolished when the Sunderland Street and Newbottle Street redevelopment took place in the late 1960s.

Staff outside the Newbottle Street Branch of the Newbottle Co-operative Society Ltd, *circa* 1930.

Wheatley's Houghton Toffee Works, *circa* 1950. The Wheatley and Gibson families were very well known for the confectionery made in their Houghton factories.

G. Stephenson, blacksmith, Durham Road, on 30th August 1957.

Below: Interior of the New Market, Newbottle Street, 1958.

A view of Newbottle Street in 2000.

Costcutter shop and post office in Hetton Road in 2000.

Mr Sangster inside his
fresh fish shop in
Newbottle Street in 1991.

Below: Mr Sangster
outside his shop in 2000.

This part of Newbottle Street, pictured in 2000, is occupied by a variety of local businesses, including: Tandoori Night Indian takeaway; K. Forster, Specialist Electrical Engineers; the Barbers; Emerald Windows and Conservatories; Derek Moss, funeral director; and K. Lydiatt & Co Ltd, plumbing, heating and sanitary engineers.

Mr Hodgkiss and staff outside Stuart Wm Hodgkiss, butchers, Newbottle Street in 2000.

Market Place Sandwiches in Nesham Place in 2000.

D.M. Colling, newsagents & licensed grocer, Gilpin Street in 2000.

Church Street newsagents in 2000.

Hartshorne newsagents in Houghton Road, 2000.

Houghton Cycles, Mautland Square, 2000.

The Thandi Food Market in Hall Lane, 2000.

Looking up towards the Mautland Square Shopping Precinct in 2000.

Mr W.F. Wright with working Clydesdale horses at Sedgeletch Farm, Sunniside, Houghton, *circa* 1942.

Threshing machine at work at Dene House Farm in 1954. The farm, which no longer exists, stood near Gillas Lane.

TRANSPORT

This sign stood on the A690 approaching Houghton from Sunderland near The Cut.

Sunderland District Tramways laying cables for the tramway in Hetton Road, *circa* 1905.

The first dual carriageway being built near Houghton Cut in the 1930s.

Police Inspector Thomas MacDonald of Houghton in a trap with Paddy the horse, *circa* 1912. Paddy was called up for service in the First World War and was unfortunately killed.

A Sunderland District Tramways Tram with the destination indicator showing 'Houghton-le-Spring', *circa* 1920.

T. Metcalfe's Removals lorry, *circa* 1948.

Durham Road Garage

Telephone: Houghton 2273

● *Automobile Engineer and Agent*
● *All Grades Petrols and Oils*
● *Greases and Car Accessories in Stock*

REPAIRS : SERVICE STATION : OVERHAULS

Cars for Hire at all Times

Frank Bennison

HOUGHTON - LE - SPRING

An advertisement for the Durham Road Garage of Frank Bennison, *circa* 1948.

HOUGHTON PIT

A view of the colliery, *circa* 1960. Although there were earlier coal workings in the area, Houghton Pit was sunk between 1823 and 1827. It re-opened in 1849 after an interval of twelve years and was the major employer in the town for many years. It closed in 1981. The colliery buildings were largely demolished and the surrounding area landscaped.

This photograph, probably taken shortly before the First World War, is captioned 'Bait Time Lads', and shows a group of Houghton miners. Joseph Davison-White, who was a member of the Salvation Army, and who is shown here in his uniform, was also a miner.

Below: The Mines' Rescue Brigade at Houghton, *circa* 1905. They are pictured fully equipped with 'Proto' breathing apparatus and canaries.

Members of Houghton Miners' Lodge with the Lodge Banner outside the Welfare Hall, *circa* 1956.

Houghton Miners' May Day March proceeding up Church Street in 1956.

An aerial view of Houghton Colliery, *circa* 1960. Note the gasometers middle left.

One reminder of the existence of the colliery is this brick building which can be seen today on the Houghton/Newbottle Road. It formerly housed an electricity sub-station serving the colliery.

CHURCHES AND CHAPELS

St Michael's and All Angels, the Parish Church of Houghton-le-Spring in 2000. Churches and chapels have played an important part in the history of the town and continue to do so. The Parish Church dates largely from the 13th century, although features from an earlier Norman church can be seen. The present tower was not constructed until the early 19th century and old prints exist showing a lower tower with a lead covered spire.

Bernard Gilpin was Rector of Houghton from 1558-83 and was known as 'the Apostle of the North'. He travelled widely to preach in the North of England and was widely respected. He refused an offer of the Bishopric of Carlisle. His stone tomb can be seen in the church and on this is carved his coat of arms which includes a wild boar.

John Barwick was Rector of Houghton from 1645-61. His appointment was barely effective because it was made during the Civil War and the Bishop who appointed him had been deprived of the necessary powers. During this period, Barwick was charged with high treason, and was committed to the Tower of London for over two years. However, when the monarchy was restored in 1660 he was appointed Dean of Durham and in 1661 became Dean of St Paul's.

IOHANNES BARWICK S.T.P.
Ecclesiæ S. Pauli Londinensis Decanus

William Sancroft was Rector from 1661-64. He was Master of Emmanuel College, Cambridge from 1662-65 and in 1664 became Dean of St Paul's when the cathedral was being rebuilt after the Great Fire. In 1677 he was appointed Archbishop of Canterbury but subsequently fell into dispute with King James II. He was one of seven bishops committed to the Tower of London in 1688 and then put on trial for seditious libel. He was found not guilty. Notwithstanding his stand against James, Sancroft felt it impossible to lawfully appoint a new sovereign even after James fled to France. In 1690, after the accession to the throne by William and Mary, he was deprived of the Archbishopric.

William Sancroft Arch Bishop of Canterbury.

After D.Loggan.

His Autograph from an Original in the Possession of John Thane.

Sir George Wheler was Rector from 1710-23. His parents had been supporters of the Royalist cause during the Civil War. On his return from a tour of Europe he received a knighthood, although only aged 17.

The Right Revᵈ Dᴿ THOMAS SECKER,
Late ARCHBISHOP of CANTERBURY.

Thomas Secker, Rector from 1723-27. He was the third Rector to later become Dean of St Paul's and the second to become Archbishop of Canterbury. Apart from being a priest he was also a doctor of medicine. He was Archbishop of Canterbury from 1758-68.

The Honourable John Grey, Rector from 1847-95. Between 1789 and 1895, a period of 106 years there were only two Rectors of Houghton – Edward Thurlow, Rector from 1789-1847, and John Grey.

Oswald Noel Gwilliam, Rector from 1948-72. He became an Honorary Canon of Durham Cathedral and will be well remembered by many readers.

Peter Brett, Rector from 1972-83. From Houghton he went to Canterbury Cathedral as a Residentiary Canon.

Peter Fisher, Rector from 1983-95 and his wife Elizabeth. After leaving Houghton he became Principal of Queen's College, Birmingham. In 2000 he was appointed an Honorary Canon of Birmingham Cathedral.

Members of the Choir of St Michael and All Angels, *circa* 1995.

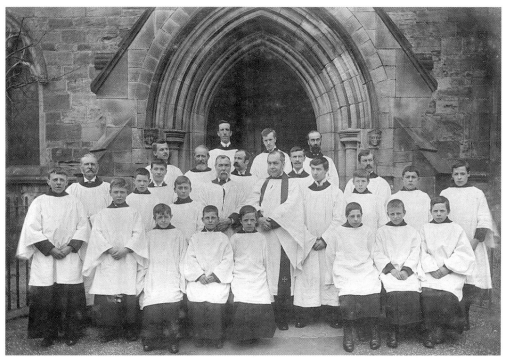

Canon Alfred Merle Norman and the Choir of St Michael and All Angels outside the church, *circa* 1895. Alfred Merle Norman was Rector from 1895-98. He was the first Rector of the new Parish of Burnmoor from 1866-95 and was a Fellow of the Royal Society.

Interior of St Mark's Mission Church, Quarry Road, approximately 1910. The Mission Church was an Anglican Church connected with the Parish Church. Quarry Row was demolished in the 1960s.

The Palm Sunday Procession to the Parish Church in 1998. The Almshouses can be seen in the background.

The Civic Service at the Parish Church in 1997. From left: the Mayor of Sunderland; The Mayoress; the High Sheriff of Tyne and Wear, Mrs S. Murray; Mr Murray; Father W. O'Gorman, Roman Catholic Parish Priest of Houghton-le-Spring; and Dr Ian Wallis, Rector of Houghton.

The Bishop of Durham, Dr David Jenkins, and the Rector of Houghton, the Reverend Peter Fisher, at the laying of the foundation stone of the new Kepier Hall building in 1991.

St Michael's Roman Catholic Church and Presbytery, Durham Road, in 2000. The church was designed in the 1830s by Ignatius Bonomi, a well known North Eastern architect, who also designed Lambton Castle.

Children's display at the Roman Catholic Church Bazaar, *circa* 1935.

Father Tuohey celebrating Holy Communion at St Michael's Roman Catholic Church in the 1960s.

The Bethany Christian Centre in Hetton Road. The new centre opened in 1997, and contains a church, meeting rooms, classrooms, a sports hall and a restaurant. The Bethany Church began in Houghton in the early 20th century and was housed at various times in Newbottle Street, Sunderland Street, Pottery Yard and Union Street. In 1965 a new church in Nesham Place was opened and this was eventually replaced by the centre in Hetton Road.

A Bethany Church Sunday School at Nesham Place in the 1980s.

The Methodist Boys' Brigade marching from the Market Place into Nesham Place, *circa* late 1940s. The shop middle left was then occupied by G. Ritchey, confectioner and fruiterer (now Market Place Sandwiches). In the middle background can just be seen Mill House, now occupied by Bailes the Printers, and one of the few Market Place buildings from that period which still stand today. Mill House Works which are attached to Mill House were once used for the manufacture of confectionery, a product for which the town was well known for many years.

The congregation in Mautland Street Methodist Church during the Houghton Methodists' Eistedfodd, 2nd November 1951.

Mautland Street Methodist Church as it is today. The present church was built in the early 1980s on the site of the previous church.

The Methodist Church, Blind Lane, in 2000, is also known as Sunniside Chapel. It opened for worship in 1899. The original church can be easily identified, although a modern extension has been added.

The Assemblies of God Eschol Church in Scott Street. The foundation stone is dated 1949.

The Kingdom Hall of Jehovah's Witnesses, Houghton Road, in 2000.

HOUGHTON IN THE FIRST AND SECOND WORLD WARS

A tank outside Robinson's Brewery, Durham Road, during the First World War.

Like the war memorials in towns and villages throughout the country, the Houghton War Memorial in the grounds of the Parish Church bears witness to the large numbers of lives lost during the First World War. In the Second World War many lives were also lost, but there is no sculptured memorial.

There will still be a significant number of Houghton people who served in the forces or worked in civilian occupations during the Second World War, and who have photographs of themselves during this period. There will be others who have photographs of relatives who served in the World Wars. These photographs are important historical records but many are being lost for ever. It is important they are retained, or donated to a military museum or archive. If there are no original details on the back, then, wherever possible, a sticker should be attached giving information about people shown, where they came from, and if they were in the forces, the name of their unit. The author of this book would be very pleased to hear from anyone about their own war record, or the war record of a member of their family, and he can be contacted at the address given at the back of this book.

Frederick Denby of Houghton, who joined the Durham Light Infantry for the duration of the First World War. He was a Prisoner of War for four years, arriving home at Christmas 1918.

Below: Soldiers marching along Church Street around 1940.

During the Second World War, Houghton itself went largely unscathed from bombing raids by the Luftwaffe, their principal target in the area being Sunderland where there were very heavy bombing raids from 1940 to 1943, with many losses of life. There are records of four high explosive bombs being dropped on Houghton Cut in July 1940, and an incendiary bomb being dropped between Houghton and Seaham in March 1943. This photograph is of Frederick Denby, the son of Frederick Denby shown on the previous page. He was a regular soldier for twenty-two years and during the Second World War saw service in France, the Middle East, North Africa and North West Europe, with the Royal Artillery.

Ben Rowell was born in Houghton and served in the Green Howards for thirty-six years. During the Second World War he saw service in Norway, Burma, Italy and North West Europe.

Nancy Rowell, who was born in Houghton, joined the ATS in 1939 and served throughout the war. After the war she remained in the Army, reaching the rank of Warrant Officer.

Thomas Rowell, who was born in Mildred Street. During the Second World War he served in the early Desert Campaigns, Burma and North West Europe, with the Hussars.

Bill Curry of Houghton who served with the Royal Navy in the Patrol Service and Minesweepers. The town had a strong connection with the Royal Navy during the Second World War as it adopted a ship, HMS *Welland*, during Warship Week in December 1941. A plaque presented by the Lords Commissioner of the Admiralty to Houghton-le-Spring Urban District Council to commemorate the adoption can be seen on the wall of one of the stairwells in the Council Offices in the Park.

George Fenton of Houghton served with 8th Battalion, Durham Light Infantry. He was taken Prisoner of War and is shown on the right in Stalag 8B.

John Gordon Robson of Houghton shown far right. He served with the Royal Engineers and took part in the Normandy Landings in 1944.

Jean Campbell of Houghton is pictured fifth left, front row, in 1944. She served with the Women's Auxiliary Air Force from 1940-46.

A tragic incident in the town during the Second World War occurred in 1941 when a Hurricane fighter tried to make an emergency landing on Houghton Golf Course. The pilot, Sergeant Frank Stamp of the Royal Canadian Air Force, unfortunately lost his life. He is pictured on the right in this photograph with his brother Henry. Mr Henry Stamp has corresponded with Mrs Moyra Coxon, the daughter of Mrs Nan Taylor who with Mrs Eva Hall were playing golf at the time, and who tried to help Sergeant Stamp.

Below: The Officers of 388 Searchlight Battery, Royal Artillery, in 1941. Captain William Brown, a Territorial Army Officer who served throughout the war, is pictured front row, third from right. Both before and after the war he was a solicitor in the Sunderland Street firm of Legge & Miller (see page 34).

SCHOOLS

A Morris Dancers Group at the Council School (better known as Newbottle Street School), *circa* 1910. The school was demolished several years ago and the site is vacant.

Schools have had a long history in Houghton, the best known for over three centuries being the Kepier School (see page 39). In Parson's & White's *History, Directory and Gazette of the County of Durham and Northumberland* published in the 1820s it is mentioned that, 'The Girls' Blue Coat School in Newbottle Lane (where 28 girls are clothed and educated, out of an estate at Rainton) was purchased with a legacy bequeathed by Sir George Wheeler Knight, and was enlarged in 1803, where twelve additional scholars now receive instruction at the expense of the ladies of Houghton, who remunerate the teacher (Eliz Foss) with an annual contribution.' Does any reader know when this school ceased to exist?

Children of William Street Weslyan School, *circa* 1905. The school and street have been long demolished.

A class with their teacher at Newbottle Street School, *circa* 1928.

Margaret Johnson, headmistress, outside of Newbottle Street School, *circa* 1930.

Children crossing the road from Newbottle Street School on 14th January 1960.

Houghton-le-Spring Sub-Committee.

EVENING CLASSES

WILL BE HELD IN THE

COUNCIL SCHOOL,

HOUGHTON-LE-SPRING,

COMMENCING

Monday, 24th September, 1917.

TIME TABLE OF CLASSES.

The Evening Classes are now graded into Courses, and Students can study specially for any particular trade or profession. All Students must attend all the Subjects in the Course.

Every intending Student must interview the Organising Teacher, Mr. THOS. S. ELLIOTT, before commencing the Classes. For this purpose the School will be open on Tuesday and Wednesday, 18th and 19th September, from 7 to 9 p.m.

Attention is drawn to the fact that the Old First Year Course has been abolished, and that an Examination will be held on 5th Sept. for those who intend to join the Classes. It is urgently necessary that Boys and Girls leaving the Elementary Schools should sit for this Examination at the earliest possible time.

It should be noted that the Names of the Grouped Courses are changed in accordance with this arrangement *e.g.* 2nd Year Commercial becomes 1st Year Commercial.

James C. Hudson, Printer, Newbottle Street, Houghton-le-Spring.

The first page of a timetable of evening classes held at the Council School, Newbottle Street, in 1917.

This part of St Michael's Roman Catholic Primary School in Durham Road
dates from about 1870 and at the time of compiling this book contains the
oldest classroom still in use in the Borough of Sunderland. This and the
remainder of the existing school is to be demolished and will be replaced by a
new school on the opposite side of Durham Road shown below during the
course of construction in 2000.

The pupils and staff of St Michael's Roman Catholic Primary School in 2000.

Class at St Michael's Roman Catholic School with teacher Mr Jack Graney in the late 1960s.

Year 7 at St Michael's Roman Catholic Primary School in 1987.

Houghton-le-Spring Grammar (or Secondary) School in the late 1940s. The school stood between Hetton Road and Durham Road and was demolished in the early 1990s, the site being developed for housing.

A view of sports day at Houghton Grammar School on 6th June 1958.

Houghton-le-Spring Secondary School cricket team in 1936. Back row:
A. Mitchell, ? McCardle, L. Ellison, J. Best, T. Race and A. Willis. Front row:
? Coombe, L. Hudson, J. Smith, W. White and F. Chesterton.

A sponsored skip at Burnside Upper Primary School in 1992. The school was
opened in 1972 and became a Primary School in 1983.

Class 5/6S at Burnside Primary School in 1999.

The whole school of Gillas Lane Primary in 2000.

Kite flying in the playground of Gillas Lane Primary School in the 1990s.

Davenport School in Durham Road. Built in the late 1960s, the school was originally known as Glebe School. It was renamed Davenport in 1988 after George Davenport, Rector of Houghton 1664-69, and in 2000 caters enthusiastically for seventy-nine children with severe and moderate learning difficulties, an increasing number having forms of autism.

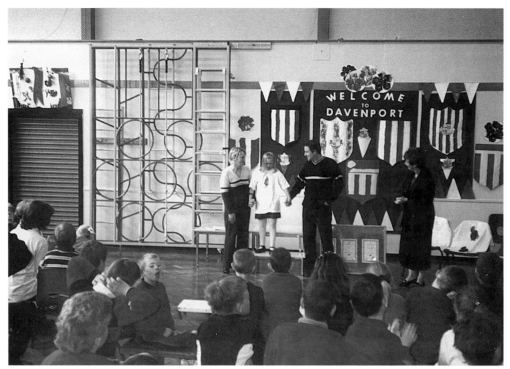

Children at Davenport School in the 1990s.

Houghton-le-Spring Modern School in the 1950s. The school was demolished following the opening of the new Kepier School in Dairy Lane. The Bernard Gilpin Primary School was built on the school's sports ground in 1993.

A class at Houghton Modern School in 1948.

The Bernard Gilpin Primary School during the course of construction in 1993.
Houghton Health Centre, which is mentioned in the celebrated series *The
Penguin Buildings of England, County Durham 2nd Edition* by Nikolaus
Pevsner revised by Elizabeth Williamson, can be seen background right.

Mr Offer, headteacher of Bernard Gilpin Primary School, with members of the 1995-96 Year 1 Group holding their maths' award certificates.

The 2000, Year 2 Group of Bernard Gilpin Primary School who devised their own Olympic Games at their awards ceremony.

MORE PEOPLE AND PLACES

A meal for elderly people held in the Welfare Hall (see page 40), *circa* 1935.

Houghton Ladies football team, 1917-18.

Houghton Branch of St John Ambulance, *circa* late 1920s.

The bar of the Newcastle Arms which stood in Newbottle Street, *circa* 1925. (See page 12.)

Houghton-le-Spring Police Division in the 1920s.

Durham Hunger March passing through Houghton in October 1936.

Leslie Jackson was the first boy from Houghton to be picked for the Durham County Schoolboys' football team. The photograph shows him in his County Cap. He went on to play professionally for Bolton, Burnley, York and Darlington. On the outbreak of the Second World War he returned to Houghton and he worked at the colliery until 1963.

The front cover of the programme for the performance of Gilbert and Sullivan's *Iolanthe* by Houghton-le-Spring and District Amateur Operatic Society at The Gaiety Theatre, Newbottle Street, on 29th October 1923. The Gaiety Theatre later became The Grand Cinema and the building is now occupied by KwikSave Supermarket.

The conductor and producer for the Operatic Society was Henry Lax, pictured here. In 1930 the *Durham County Advertiser and Chronicle* reported that although Henry Lax, 'never had a single music lesson during the whole of his life he has conducted and produced many operas, and besides this, he has officiated as an orchestral and choir conductor.' He was choirmaster at Houghton Parish Church during the First World War, and also conductor of the Houghton-le-Spring Glee Party, which during the First World War visited hospitals and gave concerts to soldiers and patients.

The Gilpin Thorn in the Rectory Park, *circa* 1955. Due to the good care of successive gardeners, the tree, a Hawthorn, which dates back to the time of Bernard Gilpin, Rector of Houghton from 1558-83, still survives. Tree surgery to keep it healthy has today altered its shape from that shown in the photograph.

These massive limestone cliffs can be seen in the old burial ground near Houghton Cut. The burial ground was opened in the 19th century, but is now disused and has been landscaped, although a few grave stones remain. In the Parish Church there is a memorial window to William Standish of Cocken Hall, near Finchale Priory, who died in 1856, after his horse fell over one of the cliffs.

The interior of Houghton Empire Cinema, Newbottle Street, in 1951 after alterations. In 1931 it advertised one show nightly, two on Saturday. Seats cost 3d to 1s 3d. The facade has been rebuilt, but the original auditorium can be clearly seen from the outside at the rear. The building retains a connection with its past, as it has been named Empire House. It is now occupied by Houghton Carpets.

Approaching Houghton along Durham Road from Rainton Bridge, *circa* 1956.

Women's Bowls at the Welfare Ground in 2000.

The Mayor and Mayoress of Sunderland at Houghton Golf Club after a Pro-Am
competition in the 1990s. The club's honorary secretary, Mr N. Wales, is
second right. The club was established in 1908. In 1914 the entry for
Houghton in a Golf Club Directory stated that there were 74 members, that
visitors were welcome at one shilling a day, there were no restrictions for
ladies, and that there was no Sunday play. In 2000 there are 679 members.

The Market Place looking towards Nesham Place in the 1960s.

Looking towards the Green and the Market Place on the Seaham Road in 2000.

The Social Club & Institute Comrades of the Great War (1914-1918) in Peartree Place before the new club house was built on the site in 1957.

Members outside the Comrades of the Great War Club in 2000.

Houghton Comrades Club Pigeon Homing Society, *circa* 1970. The Society is still very active.

Houghton Comrades Club committee, members and sports teams, *circa* 1975.

Houghton Charity Jazz Band which raised a great deal of money for worthy causes before the Second World War.

Hymn singing at Houghton Feast in Coronation Year, 8th October 1953. Note the illuminated royal emblem on the Old Rectory. Community singing at Houghton Feast was a popular feature and continued outside until the mid 1970s. Houghton Feast, which has been taking place since the Middle Ages, was established as a festival of the dedication of the Parish Church of St Michael. By custom it is held on 10th October if a Sunday, otherwise on the preceding Sunday, and it now continues for a week. Parson & White in their 1820s *History, Directory & Gazette of the County of Durham and Northumberland* reported that, '… the town becomes crowded with strangers at an early hour. The Festival continues with great excess for three or four days during which period there are horse races, and various other amusements.'

Another scene of community singing at Houghton Feast, *circa* 1974.

Horse racing at Houghton Feast on 13th October 1938. This was the last year in which horse racing was held.

Greyhound racing was held during the Feast for a number of years after the Second World War for the Houghton Feast Greyhound Handicap.

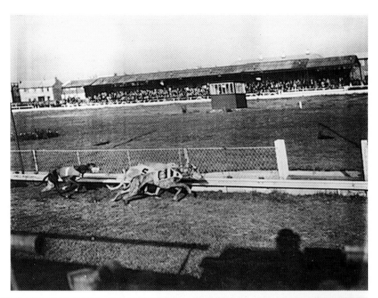

The fair held in the Market Place at Houghton Feast in the mid 1950s. The Wheatsheaf Inn on left was still in use as a public house and some of the older Market Place buildings can also be seen. The photograph was taken before the building of the new Local Authority housing in the later 1950s. In the far right background can just be seen Field House Farm. Before and after the Second World War the Feast was visited by a caravan mobile school for showmen's children run by 'Auntie' Brown, the widow of an Anglican clergyman.

On the Waltzer at Houghton Feast, 9th October 1959. In recent years the fair has been held on the field in Dairy Lane next to the park.

A tradition of Houghton Feast is the roasting of the ox which is now undertaken by Houghton Rotary Club. Money raised from the sale of beef sandwiches is given to charity.

The fair at Houghton Feast in 1963. It was then held on 'The Lake'. (See page 1.)

Houghton Feast Show at Houghton Sports Complex, 14th October 2000. The event, which is held over two days, is sponsored by the *Sunderland Echo*, and organised by Sunderland City Contracting Services, Parks, Open Spaces & Ground Maintenance. Exhibits include a wide variety of vegetables and flowers, and prizes are awarded.

Houghton Fire Station and Mines' Rescue Centre at the Gillas Lane and Hetton Road crossroads, *circa* 1925. Note the wooden signpost.

Members of the Fire Brigade outside Houghton Fire Station, *circa* 1935.

Houghton Fire Station and Mines' Rescue Centre in the late 1940s. Note the absence of traffic lights in the photograph, and then compare it with the photograph below.

The Fire Station Buildings in 2000. They continue to be occupied by the Mines' Rescue Service although they no longer house the Fire Brigade.

A street party in the Market Place to celebrate the Coronation of George VI in 1937.

Houghton-le-Spring Enterprise Centre occupies the site of 'The Lake' on the aptly named Lake Road. Provided by Sunderland City Council, the centre contains small low cost units for industrial and office use, and offers secretarial and administrative services. There are also exhibition and conference facilities.

A Costume Pageant parading to the Parish Church, *circa* 1950. The First World War Memorial is on the right, and in the background is the stone building in Church Street where Dunelm Granite, Monumental Masons had their works.

Dunelm Granite's Works were demolished and the site now forms the entrance to Houghton Health Centre.

A view of The Broadway in the early 1950s. St Michael's Church Hall, left, and the Old Rectory wall, centre, have been long demolished.

Houghton Hall in 1999. The Hall is generally believed to have been built by Robert Hutton, a supporter of Parliament in the Civil War, and a grandson of Robert Hutton, Rector of Houghton, 1589-1623. As the photograph shows, the building is now boarded up. Before its closure it had been used as a social club and also by Houghton-le-Spring YMCA.

This photograph is believed to have been taken at a dinner of the Houghton Men's Fellowship in the late 1950s, and some readers will know precisely. Canon O.N. Gwilliam, Rector of Houghton, is shown front row, second left.

Houghton-le-Spring and District Centre for the Blind, near Thornhill Street, was built in 1955. Two foundation stones were laid, one by Lady Serena James, although the inscription has completely worn away; and the other, where the inscription is still legible, by Councillor T.W. Urwin, Chairman of the Council, who later became MP for Houghton-le-Spring.

Crushing gravel in The Cut early in the 20th century. The hills through which The Cut has been formed consist of dolomite, a limestone, which has been quarried mainly for building purposes.

The quarry of Houghton Limeworks Limited in 1948. In an announcement that year the company said that their dolomite could be, '... used for boiler lagging, pipe covering; and the manufacture of rubber tyres; and that toothpaste, cosmetics, dolls, dyes, fireworks, colouring of cigarette and other papers etc, rely on dolomite for their manufacture.'

Bibliography

Houghton-le-Spring Official Guide 1947
The Dictionary of National Biography
Piggot's Directory of County Durham
Who's Who
Parson & White, *History, Directory & Gazette of The County of Durham and Northumberland*
Pevsner N. Revised by E. Williamson, *The Penguin Buildings of England, County Durham 2nd Edition*
Richardson K., *Houghton-le-Spring and Hetton-le-Hole in Old Photographs*
Richardson K., *Houghton-le-Spring and Hetton-le-Hole in Old Photographs – A Second Selection*
Surtees R., *The History and Antiquities of the County Palatine of Durham*
Dowding B., *Durham Mines: Names and dates of Coalworkings in County Durham*
Whelan's Durham Township Directory
Who's Who of British Members of Parliament published by Harvester Press, Sussex, and Humanities Press, New Jersey

If you would like to contact the author, please write to:

Geoffrey Berriman
Garden Cottage
Lambton Park
Chester-le-Street
Co. Durham
DH3 4PN

Back cover: A view of the White Lion in 1905 with a tram leaving for Fence Houses.

The People's History

To receive a catalogue of our latest titles – send a large SAE to:

The People's History Ltd
Suite 1, Byron House
Seaham Grange Business Park
Seaham, County Durham
SR7 0PY